Butch
The Outdoor Cat

Diane DeFord

Illustrated by Pam Posey

Dominie Press, Inc.

The development of the *Carousel Readers* was supported by the Reading Recovery project at California State University, San Bernardino. All authors' royalties from the sale of the *Carousel Readers* will be used to support various Reading Recovery projects.

Publisher: Raymond Yuen
Illustrator: Pam Posey
Cover Designer: Pamela Pettigrew-Norquist

Published by

 Dominie Press, Inc.
5945 Pacific Center Boulevard
San Diego, California 92121 USA

ISBN 1-56270-259-9
Printed in Singapore by PH Productions.

2 3 4 5 6 7 PH 98 97 96 95

Butch is an outdoor cat.

When the spring sun shines,
he stretches in the sun,

and swats at big black flies.

When the summer grass
is high, he hides,

and surprises his enemies.

When autumn leaves
start to fall,

he chases them
across the lawn.

But when the winter rain
and snow fall,

Butch stops, and looks inside...

and begs to be
an indoor cat.